"Here are strange marls, the relics of infinite animal life, into which has sunk the lizard of the dragon of antiquity—the gigantic *Hadrosaurus*, who cranes his snaky throat at us in the museum, swelling with the tale of immemorial times when he weltered here in the sunny ooze."

Lippincott's Magazine of Popular Literature and Science, 1873

Throughout much of the nineteenth century, fossil hunting was a gentlemen's hobby. Curious fossil hunters, like William Foulke, searched for and, on occasion, found huge fossilized bones—but they could only speculate on their origin. No one knew what a dinosaur looked like, or if they ever really existed, because a complete skeleton had never been found.

Lanterns lit the way as farmer John Hopkins and fossil hunter William Foulke made their way through the fog. They were searching for an old dig site where Mr. Hopkins had once dug up mysterious bones. "Strange and monstrous bones!" exclaimed the farmer. "No head was found. Only large vertebrae, except one that resembled a gigantic shoulder blade."

As a marl farmer, Mr. Hopkins dug up his organic-rich soil, called marl, and sold it as fertilizer. His workers had found the bones while digging twenty years earlier. At the time, he had no interest in the bones and he gave them away as curiosities. People used them as doorstops and to prop open windows.

Perhaps, thought William, more bones lay buried. With Mr. Hopkins's permission, William hired a crew of marl diggers. Day after day, they dug down through thick slimy clay.

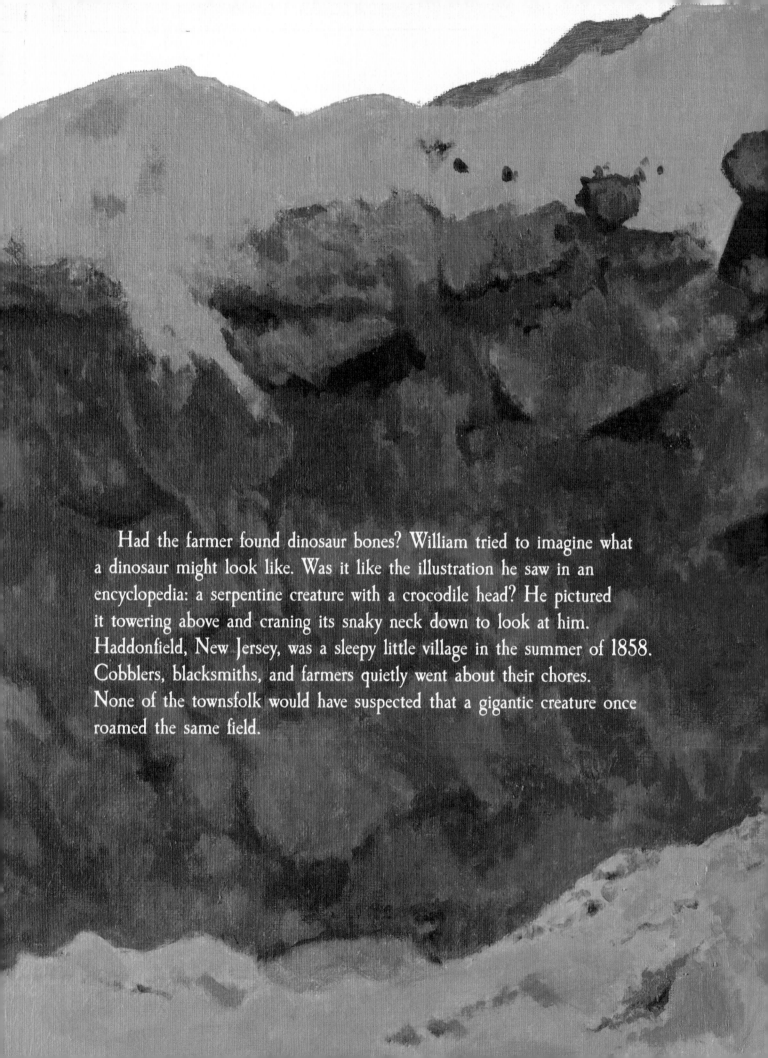

Had the farmer found dinosaur bones? William tried to imagine what a dinosaur might look like. Was it like the illustration he saw in an encyclopedia: a serpentine creature with a crocodile head? He pictured it towering above and craning its snaky neck down to look at him. Haddonfield, New Jersey, was a sleepy little village in the summer of 1858. Cobblers, blacksmiths, and farmers quietly went about their chores. None of the townsfolk would have suspected that a gigantic creature once roamed the same field.

Four feet down, William came across a layer of decomposed seashells and decayed pieces of wood. Sifting the marl through small metal screens, he occasionally found what appeared to be shark's teeth. Ankle deep in gray slime, he raked over the soil to make sure he did not miss anything, but no bones were evident.

Eight weeks later, there was still no sign of any strange and monstrous bones. The pit was now nearly eight feet deep. William scooped up a handful of marl and let it fall between his now calloused fingers. The harder he worked, the more he wondered: are the remains of a dinosaur really down there?

As summer turned to fall, William continued to dig. Above, the wind whistled past. It sounded, he thought, like a dinosaur groaning its last breath. He brushed away sediment, exposing a shiny, black rock. Or was it a fossil? He wiped his brow and brushed again, exposing what appeared to be small vertebrae. Hurriedly, he dug deeper. "Fragments of a jaw!" he muttered in astonishment. The further he dug, the more remains were exposed, until a pile of ebony bones lay before him.

William had never seen anything like them. He tried to imagine the beast again. This time it was bulky and stood upright with huge legs and a massive tail. He sketched and recorded the measurements of each bone. He tried to guess what each fossil might be. Perhaps this is part of a hip, he thought. Another looked like a large vertebra.

William transported the bones back to his residence. He placed each one out on the floor. He knew they were extraordinary. But just what had he found? The fossils were too big to even have once belonged to an elephant. One fossil, appearing to be a thighbone, was heavy and measured forty inches in length and nine inches wide. Another was nearly as massive, measuring thirty-six and a half inches by eleven inches.

The next morning, William wrote a letter to his friend Dr. Joseph Leidy at the Academy of Natural Sciences in Philadelphia. Leidy was an expert on anatomy and on vertebrate paleontology. He requested that Dr. Leidy come at once. "I have taken some splendid bones from the marl," wrote William. "The fruits are abundant and I wish them to be preserved for science."

Dr. Leidy, along with his associate Isaac Lea, promptly took the Vine Street ferry to New Jersey, where they boarded a passenger train to Haddonfield. William met them at the station, and by carriage they made their way down Main Street to William's residence. Upon his arrival, Dr. Leidy recognized immediately that the bones were those of a dinosaur.

The excavation continued expanding the site to encompass an area sixteen by eight feet. More fossils were uncovered. With a small trowel and knife, Dr. Leidy carefully removed each fragmented fossil from its clay home. When it appeared that nothing further could be excavated, the dig was discontinued. Forty-nine bones and teeth were brought back to the Academy for further study. At the time, it was the most complete dinosaur skeleton ever discovered.

The sleepy little village of Haddonfield, New Jersey, did not seem so sleepy anymore. William imagined the monstrous beast lifting its massive head and swinging its giant tail from side to side. It bellowed and grunted. It roared! Its footsteps pounded the earth: the very same earth that William now walked. It was hard to believe. Dr. Leidy named the dinosaur *Hadrosaurus foulkii* after William. In Latin it means "Foulke's bulky lizard."

Ten years later, British sculptor Benjamin Waterhouse
Hawkins created plaster casts of the bones and assembled
them into a realistic skeleton. With only forty-nine
bones to work with and the skull missing, the
skeleton was approximated. No one knew that
the kangaroo-like stance and the skull
shaped like an iguana's were inaccurate.
Nonetheless, it was the first
mounted dinosaur displayed in
the world.

Paleontologists today believe that the *Hadrosaurus* held its tail aloft and its upper body forward to move in a manner similar to a bird. It weighed as much as four tons and grew to lengths of twenty-five feet and as tall as nine feet. It traveled in herds, laid eggs in nests, and could rear up on its hind legs to run or to feed on vegetation. Although a land dweller, the *Hadrosaurus* was a good swimmer and roamed the swamps and wooded areas along the shore. It is a member of the dinosaur family known as the "duckbills" because of its birdlike jaw and skull. It lived during the Late Cretaceous Period, approximately 80 million years ago.

Haddonfield, NJ.

In the Late Cretaceous Period, most of southern New Jersey sat under a hundred feet of seawater. It is assumed that the *Hadrosaurus foulkii* died somewhere near the coastline, which at the time was the region now recognized as Philadelphia, Pennsylvania. Its remains washed out to sea and settled miles away in what is now called Haddonfield, New Jersey. Over time, the bones were covered up with mud and decaying sea life, creating an ancient lagoon or shore-like sediment called marl. The fossils lay there for millions of years, waiting to be unearthed.

William's discovery proved that dinosaurs existed, ending years of speculation. It changed paleontology from a gentlemen's hobby to a mainstream science. His dig site lingered in obscurity for over a hundred years. In 1984, thirteen-year-old Haddonfield resident and Eagle Scout Christopher Brees read about the nearly forgotten discovery in a magazine. He researched the site and placed a stone plaque marking Foulke's find. It is now called Hadrosaurus Park. In 1988, fourth-grade teacher Joyce Berry and her students at Strawbridge Elementary School in Haddon Township proposed to the New Jersey legislature that *Hadrosaurus foulkii* be named the state dinosaur. In 1991, it was officially designated the state dinosaur. In 1994, William's dig site was designated a National Historic Landmark. To commemorate the event, sculptor John Giannotti created a bronze statue of the dinosaur eight feet tall and fifteen feet long, nicknamed Haddy.

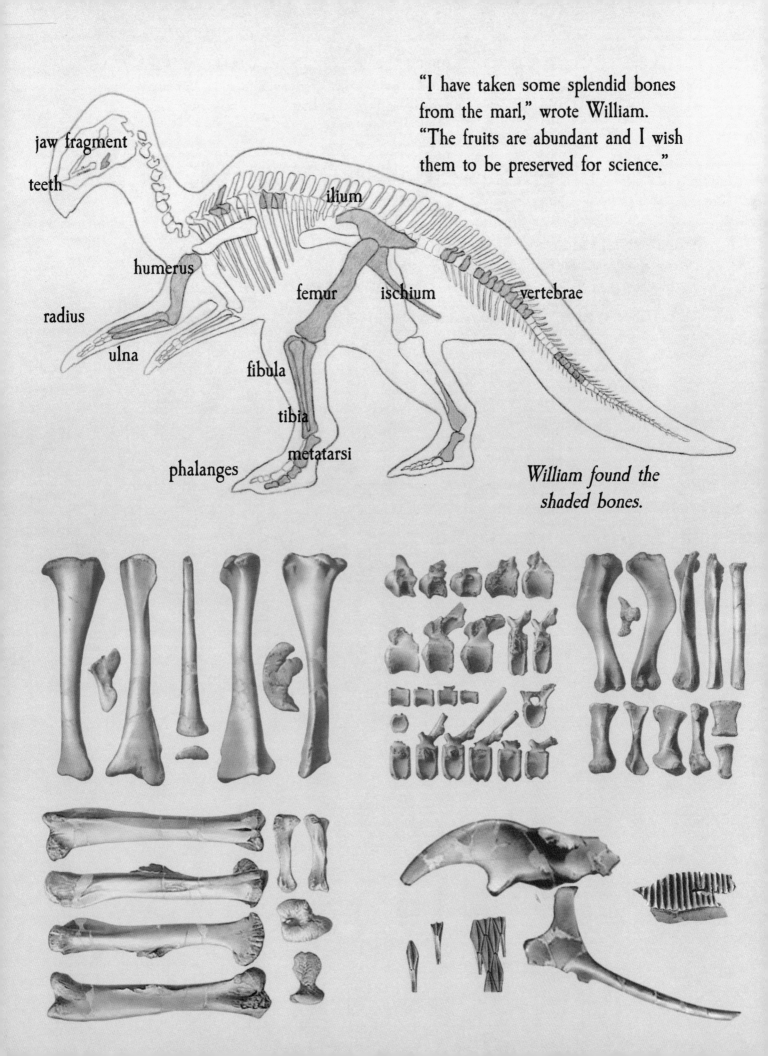

jaw fragment

teeth

humerus

radius

ulna

ilium

femur   ischium   vertebrae

fibula

tibia

phalanges   metatarsi

"I have taken some splendid bones
from the marl," wrote William.
"The fruits are abundant and I wish
them to be preserved for science."

*William found the
shaded bones.*

The author gratefully acknowledges paleontologist Dr. Ted Daeschler and Library Director Danianne Mizzy at the Academy of Natural Sciences in Philadelphia, Pennsylvania. He would also like to thank DeForest Butch Brees, Katherine M. Tassini of the Historical Society of Haddonfield, and Jo-Ann Pure of the Haddonfield Library for their cooperation.

For Kevin Jr., Juliette, Allison, Wyatt, and Charlotte

SELECTED BIBLIOGRAPHY

Account of the Remains of Fossil Extinct Reptile Recently Discovered at Haddonfield, New Jersey
From the Proceedings of the Academy of Natural Sciences of Philadelphia, Dec. 1858

Original Letters Written by William Parker Foulke to Dr. Leidy, 1858
Ewell Sale Stewart Library
Academy of Natural Sciences

William Parker Foulke Papers
Ca. 1840-1865
American Philosophical Society
105 South Fifth Street
Philadelphia, Pennsylvania 19106-3386

PLACES TO VISIT

Hadrosaurus Park
Maple Avenue
Haddonfield, New Jersey 08033
www.hadrosaurus.com/hadropark.shtml

Haddy the Dinosaur
2 Kings Court
Haddonfield, New Jersey 08033
www.hadrosaurus.com

The Academy of Natural Sciences
1900 Benjamin Franklin Parkway
Philadelphia, Pennsylvania 19103
www.ansp.org

Made in the USA
Charleston, SC
22 December 2015